J. G Van Ryn

Disestablishment a Duty

An Appeal to the Conscience

J. G Van Ryn

Disestablishment a Duty
An Appeal to the Conscience

ISBN/EAN: 9783337034993

Printed in Europe, USA, Canada, Australia, Japan

Cover: Foto ©Thomas Meinert / pixelio.de

More available books at **www.hansebooks.com**

DISESTABLISHMENT A DUTY,

An Appeal to the Conscience.

BY

J. G. VAN RYN.

"SEARCH THE SCRIPTURES."

LONDON:
JOHN SNOW & CO., IVY LANE, PATERNOSTER ROW.
1875.

CONTENTS.

	PAGE
DISESTABLISHMENT A QUESTION OF DUTY	4
DISESTABLISHMENT—WHAT IT IS	5
DISESTABLISHMENT NO DESTRUCTION OF THE CHURCH . .	6
DISESTABLISHMENT NO SPOLIATION OF THE CHURCH . .	7
DISESTABLISHMENT NO WAY TO AN ATHEISTIC STATE . .	8
DISESTABLISHMENT NO WAY TO HIERARCHICAL DOMINION OVER THE STATE	9
DISESTABLISHMENT NO DISPARAGEMENT OF THE TRUE SUPREMACY OF THE CROWN	9
DISESTABLISHMENT A REMOVAL OF WHAT IS AGAINST THE FUNDAMENTAL PRINCIPLES OF CHRIST'S KINGDOM .	10
DISESTABLISHMENT A REMOVAL OF WHAT COUNTERACTS THE WORKING OF GOD'S SPIRIT IN THE HEARTS OF BELIEVING CHURCH-PEOPLE	55
DISESTABLISHMENT A REMOVAL OF AN IMPEDIMENT TO THE COMING OF GOD'S KINGDOM IN THE WORLD . . .	72
APPEAL TO CHURCH-PEOPLE AND DISSENTERS . . .	78

DISESTABLISHMENT A DUTY.

The question of the disestablishment of the State-Church of England has, both by Churchmen and Dissenters, been regarded too much as a political party-question, and under the influence of passionate feelings, aroused by the consciousness that the dearest personal interests were at stake.

Both these tendencies, to a certain extent, are fully justified. Disestablishment means what the one side considers as destructive of the most influential safeguards of England's religion and English society, the most sacred heirloom of their fathers for centuries, interwoven with the most cherished privileges and sympathies for themselves and their children; and what the other side holds to be the final triumph of the principles of liberty of conscience and spiritual religion, in the assertion of which their fathers have suffered loss of goods, liberty, and even life, and to labour for the removal of what subjects them and their families in their daily life to all the vexations of social ostracism, and which divides English society in two hostile camps, continually engaged in mutual warfare. How can it be possible, that disestablishment, so intimately connected with the interests of all concerned, should not rouse the deepest feelings? And as the question of the connection of the English Episcopal Church with the *State* can only be decided by law, and reaches the very core of the principles of the different political parties, it is only natural that it should be considered as a political party-question of the highest importance.

But the question of disestablishment is more. It is closely connected with the very life of an important part of the *Church*—that is, of the body of Christ. It ought, therefore, above all to be regarded in the light of, and decided by, the will of Christ. The chief question ought to be: Is the establishment of the Church by the State approved or disapproved by Him? Is it in harmony with, or in opposition against, His Word, the principles of His kingdom and the dictates of His Spirit? Does it help or hinder the influence of Christ in the Church and in the world? In other words, disestablishment ought chiefly to be discussed, not on worldly principles, nor in the passionate mood and tone, commonly adopted in questions of convenience and party; but under the influence of Christ's Spirit, as a solemn question of duty, on which every one connected therewith ought to know what to think and what to do, shall he stand in a right relation to Christ and His Church.

Before, however, considering the question of disestablishment in this light, it is necessary to define clearly what is meant by it, and to remove from it carefully what is often unnecessarily mixed up with it, chiefly in the minds of the best kind of Churchpeople. Disestablishment is understood to involve a great deal more than disendowment. The Rev. Mr. Hole, in Peek's Prize Essays,* states that an established Church is the Church established in legal possession of the ancient ecclesiastical endowments of the country. But this is certainly not the full historical sense in which the Episcopal Church of England is an established Church. The royal assent to the Canons of 1604 speaks of the *present estate and government* of the Church of England by the laws of this our realm now settled and established ; Canon 3, of the *form of worship* in the Church of England, established by law and contained in the Book of Common Prayer ; Act 3, 4 Anne, for the effectual securing the kingdom of England from the apparent danger that may arise from several Acts lately passed in the Parliament of Scotland, s. 12,† " of the *liturgy, rites, ceremonies, discipline or government* of the Church as by law

---

* Peek's "Prize Essays," Octavo Edition, p. 4.
† Conf. Gibson, "Codex Juris Ecclesiastici Anglicani," Oxford, 1761, p. 20.

established;" Act 6 Anne, cap. 5, of the Protestant *religion* professed and established by law in the Church of England; of Acts of Parliament now in force for the establishment and preservation of the Church of England, and *the doctrine, worship, discipline and government* thereof. The same terms are also used in the Act of Union of England and Scotland, 5 Anne, c. 8. From these and other sources, it may be concluded that disestablishment may fairly be said to mean the legal act whereby the special connection which exists between the State and the Episcopal Church of England, as established by law, is broken; whereby, therefore, the State surrenders to that Church the special legislative, administrative, and judicial powers with respect to her doctrine, worship, discipline, and government with which the law invests the different departments of its government, and takes from the Church the special advantages, financial and otherwise, with which the law has endowed her in her character as a State-Church.

From this point of view, it is at once apparent how groundless is the apprehension of many Churchmen that disestablishment would mean the annihilation of the Episcopal Church in England. The Episcopal Church in Ireland is not annihilated by her recent disestablishment. She exists now as well as when she was an established Church; only one of her qualities, that of being established by law, has disappeared; but her existence as a Christian Church, her foundation in Christ, her life through the Holy Ghost, her means of grace, her faith, her love, her pastoral and missionary labours, are now as safe as ever. And even while through her disestablishment the regulation of her interests and her government is transferred to herself, her disestablishment impels her to a greater exertion of the powers which she possesses as a Christian Church. The prosperous condition of many of the Nonconformist Churches at home; the ample provision of Church-accommodation and the healthy life of many churches of the most differing denominations all over the United States of America, give abundant proof that the existence and prosperity of a Christian Church depend in nowise on the official support which a civil government can give to it.

Neither does disestablishment imply an enormous spoliation of property of the Church. Disestablishment includes disendowment, but disendowment does not mean spoliation. While maintaining the principle that the endowments which the Episcopal Church of England has received from the State have to be surrendered, it excludes not in the least from its application the most scrupulous respect of the right of property which the Episcopal Church of England possesses from other sources than her connection with the State; nor even a generous regard to the equal claims of those who are in the actual enjoyment of State-endowments.

Nor had the fear any solid ground that in consequence of disestablishment the State being without a State-Church would become without religion, an atheistic State. Disestablishment, as described, has to do with the legal establishment of religion by the State, not with the duty of the State in all its affairs of honouring and obeying God, who is the supreme King over the whole earth and the only Source of all true authority, wisdom, and blessing. It breaks the bond which connects the State with one sect, but it leaves in full force the moral and religious influence of the whole Church on the nation and all State-officers, to make them act as Christians in all their relations to the State, as well as the full opportunity of acknowledging God and His will in the administration of the oath; in the opening with prayer of State-assemblies and State-ceremonies; in the maintenance of the sanctification of the Sunday; in the application on legislative, administrative, and judicial domains of the principles of strict righteousness and pure morality; in the moral support of the cause of liberty of conscience, of violated rights of mankind, and of enlightened Christian religion all over the world, and in numberless other ways at home and abroad. Nowhere is Church and State more thoroughly separated than in the United States of North America, but that does not hinder the State from upholding the sanctity of the oath and of the Sunday, of opening their legislative assemblies with prayer, of holding national days of thanksgiving and fasting, and of being influenced by the principles of Christianity in their laws and institutions as far as public opinion and the individual lawgivers and State-officers are under the power of these principles.

Nor, on the other hand, will disestablishment conduce to the subjection of the State under the dominion of an ecclesiastical hierarchy. Here also the example of the United States proves that objection to be without foundation. No trace of hierarchical domination over the State is to be found there. And the ever-increasing control over the State and all its affairs by the thoroughly Protestant people of England, with their jealous care for their liberties, their mighty different Church-organizations, all on the same footing when disestablishment shall have destroyed the legal connection of one of them with the State, eagerly intent on vindicating their own rights and watching one another's doings, with their free press and their free gatherings, would render it impossible that the monstrous claims of a mediæval Papacy would be promoted in England by the disestablishment of the Episcopal Church.

Nor, lastly, does disestablishment include any disparagement of the exalted dignity and the beneficial influence of the Crown. Of course, disestablishment cannot exercise any influence on the most devoted attachment and the most loyal respect for the supremacy of the Crown in the civil, political, military, naval and international sphere. The unquestionable loyalty of many millions of Nonconformists among the Queen's subjects places this beyond doubt. But even in the ecclesiastical sphere disestablishment, though removing from the Crown what does not belong to it, the *jus in Sacra*, the dominion over all that belongs to the domain of God's Spirit in the Church; still it leaves the *jus circa Sacra* intact, the supremacy of the Crown over all ecclesiastical persons, institutions and influences, to watch that nothing detrimental to the interests of the State shall exist, in the sense that all these subjects are under the authority of civil law, guarded by the power of the judicial courts, in all that pertains to the proper domain of the State.

After having removed from disestablishment what is especially objectionable, but has really nothing to do with it, there can remain no reasonable doubt that disestablishment, in the indicated sense, is according to Christ's will, because the connection of the Church with the State, which it dissolves, is against the fundamental principles of His kingdom, counteracts the working of God's Spirit in the hearts of believing Church-people, and is an impediment to the coming of God's kingdom in the world.

I.

Disestablishment is according to Christ's will, because the connection of the Church with the State, which it dissolves, is against the fundamental principles of His kingdom.

The chief principle of the kingdom of heaven is that Christ is its King, whom the Father has elevated "far above all principalities and power and might and dominion and every name that is named, not only in this world, but also in that which is to come, and has put all things under His feet, and gave Him to be the Head over all things to the Church, which is His body, the fulness of Him that filleth all in all" (Eph. i. 20-23). But the connection of the Church with the State, in giving to the State legislative, administrative, and judicial power over the doctrine, the worship, the discipline and the government of Christ's body, is an actual denial of that sovereign dignity of Christ. It subjects Christ's Church in its deepest spiritual life, that is, while and so far as Christ lives in His Church (Gal. ii. 20; Eph. iii. 17-20; 1 Cor. xii. 12), Christ Himself under a power of this world. It assumes to bring the life, the impulses, the light, the guidance, the power of Christ's Spirit, dwelling and working in the Church (John xiv. 16, 17; xvi. 7, 12-15; Rom. viii. 9-17; 1 Cor. xii.), under the control and, in some cases, under the check of a body of men, who, as a rule, in their character as statesmen, are well qualified for their work and an honour to the English name, but of whom no worldliness, no impiety, no immorality, no infidelity, are excluded, and who have therefore no guarantee of qualification for the exercise of authority over the spiritual interests of the Church. While Christ claims to be the only Lord of His Church (Matt. xxiii. 8, 10; Acts ii. 36; 1 Cor. viii. 6; xii. 3; Eph. iv. 5; v. 23, 24; Rom. xiv. 7-9; Philip. ii. 9-11), attributes the law to the Crown, in consequence of the connection of the Church with the State, jurisdictions, privileges, superiorities and pre-eminences, spiritual and ecclesiastical over the Church,* in terms which—though the constant practice has proved them ineffective, though the enlightened piety of the present noble occupant of the throne, and the most cherished convictions of the whole nation make their becoming effective impossible—according to the rules of honest interpretation, include even the power formerly exercised in this realm by the Pope.† While Christ claims His will to be the only law of His Church (John x. 27; Luke xiv. 26, 27); His Word the only test of His truth (Luke ix. 35; John viii. 31, 32; xii. 48); His Spirit the only guide of His Church in all her affairs (John xvi. 13; Rom. viii. 14; Gal. v. 25); His influence the only authority to which His Church in her Church-character is subjected (Eph. v. 24), confers the connection of the Church with the State legislative authority over the Church's

---

* Conf. Act. i., Elizabeth 1, s. 17.

† The terms used in 1 Elizabeth 1, s. 17, "of such jurisdictions, privileges, superiorities, and pre-eminences, spiritual and ecclesiastical, *as by any spiritual or ecclesiastical power or authority hath heretofore been or may lawfully be exercised or used*" (Gibson, "Cod. Jur. Eccl.," p. 44), do not allow any other interpretation than that the powers, actually exercised by the Pope, are set beside those which he lawfully might have exercised.

doctrine, form of worship, discipline, and government in the hands of a Parliament, which consists, partly of men who do not acknowledge the rule, the word, the Spirit, the authority of Christ, and that in its deliberations and decisions with regard to the Church's affairs, is led mainly by political considerations, and not by the principles of the kingdom of heaven.

Several objections generally made against this argument are without ground.

It is said that obedience to them in authority and honouring the king are undoubtedly Christ's commandment to His Church, and that it is, therefore, manifest that it cannot interfere with Christ's kingly authority. Why then should submission of the Church in Church-matters to the State be against that authority? But the two cases are dissimilar. While there can be no doubt that the State-powers are of God, and have authority in all matters which concern the State (Rom. xiii. 1-7; 1 Peter ii. 13-17), there is no proof whatever that God has given to them any authority over the affairs of His Church. The precepts of the New Testament, which enjoin the duty of honouring the king, of being subject to the higher powers, etc., were given with respect to the heathen Roman emperors and their delegates, such as Nero and his associates, who were the enemies of the Church, who commanded, in Church matters, denial of Christ, and claimed divine honour to the Cæsars. It is clear, therefore, that these commandments have respect only to the domain of the State; while with respect to the domain of the Church the New Testament imposes the rule: "We ought to obey God rather than men," and prescribes a form of government adapted to the spiritual nature of the Church as the body of Christ, entirely distinct from all State-authorities (Eph. iv.; 1 and 2 Tim. and Titus, *passim*). Nor can the exercise of Church-authority by State-powers be defended by appealing to the Commonwealth of Israel under the Old Testament, for the Commonwealth of Israel was exceptionally theocratic, with State- and Church-laws, directly given by God; with the prophetic Spirit and the Urim and Thummim of the high priest to direct the king in his influence on the Church, and even there the management of religious affairs was in a large measure exercised by the priests and not by the king or the elders.

No solid ground, therefore, for the exercise of legislative, administrative, or judicial powers over the Church in her Church-character by State-authorities can be found in the Bible. It originated in the autocratical tendencies of Constantine the Great. It was continued in the sixteenth century in the countries whose princes were favourable to, or even the chief promoters of, Reformatory principles, in order to be able to overcome the common foe, the Romish hierarchy. But Divine authority for State-authority over Church-matters there is none. Nor is there in the nature of the case anything that justifies the extension of the commandments, given by Christ to the members of His Church in their capacity of citizens of the State, to pay conscientious obedience to the State-authorities in all matters which belong to the domain of the State, to all that belongs to the domain of the Church—that is, to all their obligations, which, as citizens of the kingdom of heaven, they have with regard to that kingdom. Both spheres are entirely different. The interests of the State, the secular commonwealth, have respect to this world, and are consequently of a civil, social, financial, political nature, to be regulated by considerations and influences in accordance with their special nature, therefore quite under the reach of the men who are at the head of the State. But the interests of the Church have respect to the salvation of the soul and the kingdom of heaven, of which Christ is the only Author and sovereign Head. Christ Himself is the Truth, which He has revealed in His Word; through the influence of His Spirit He leads His Church to understand and appropriate it. Every man who, without the supreme guidance of His Spirit, assumes to dictate what the Church has to believe, encroaches upon Christ's domain, and insults His sovereign majesty. Through His grace He moves the members of His Church to dedicate themselves unreservedly to Him, to do what, by His Spirit through His Word, He reveals in their conscience as His will, without regard to outward authority, only because it is the will of Him whom God has appointed to be their Lord, and who has bought them with His blood. Every man who seeks to bring the members of Christ's Church, in anything that regards their relation to the kingdom of heaven, under the yoke of outward authority, encroaches upon Christ's domain and insults His sovereign majesty. Through His Spirit He moves the members of His Church to pray, to worship, to praise God according to His will, in spirit and in truth. Every man who imposes by law on the Church the forms of prayer, worship, and praise which they must use, encroaches upon Christ's domain and insults His sovereign majesty. Unto Christ is committed all judgment over His Church, which He exercises in the present dispensation through the power of His Spirit and His Truth in the consciences of His people, and as far as it has to be applied in Church-discipline, through human agencies, led by His Spirit and bound to the dictates of His Word. Every man who assumes judicial authority over Christ's Church, in the spirit and according to the dictates of human laws, made without supreme regard to Christ's Word, encroaches on Christ's domain and insults His sovereign majesty.

According to Christ's will, therefore, obedience is due to State-powers, with regard to all matters belonging to the domain of the State, but not in respect to what belongs to the kingdom of heaven.

Nor is the objection valid, that every sect acknowledge in their Church-officers human agencies, who perform what in the established Church of England is delegated to the State ; that Christ Himself in His Word approves of these agencies, and that therefore it is unjust to describe the powers which the State exerts over the Episcopal Church in England as an insult to Christ's sovereign majesty. For while the human agencies, approved in the New Testament, are officers, prepared for their office through the *charisma* of Christ's Spirit (1 Cor. xii. 4-11, 28; Eph. iv. 11; 2 Cor. iii. 5, 6); the State officers are chosen without decisive regard to their relation to Christ. While the New Testament Church-officers regard themselves as servants of the Church, who eagerly claim not to be lords over God's heritage, but ensamples to the flock (1 Peter v. 3), the State-powers claim the same lordly authority over the Church, which they lawfully exercise over the State. While the New Testament Church-officers act in the name and under the authority of the Spirit, and in accordance with the Word of Christ, and have a right to acknowledgment, because Christ acts through them, the State-powers act on the authority and upon the dictates of State-laws, made and executed without supreme regard to Christ's will.

Without doubt, the Church and the State are closely connected, while the members of the Church are also members of the State;* they have several duties with respect to one another—the Church to give a hearty example of conscientious obedience to all lawful State-powers; to stand before God in behalf of the State and its interests; to be an earnest witness for the practical recognition of God and His will in all State-affairs, both by magistrates and people; to use their influence to make piety and integrity regarded as essential qualities in representatives and State-officers; and to be the salt of the nation, that promotes the religious and moral life through which alone a nation can be preserved from ruin; the State, conscious that it is its duty to acknowledge God and His will, that it has its authority from God, and that its prosperity depends on God's blessing, to honour the Church in the different denominational Church-organizations, as an instrumentality to promote the fear of God, and thereby the stability and prosperity of the State; to extend to the Church the protection which the State gives to all corporations acknowledged by it, and to watch over the Church, that no harm to

* This is quite different from the argument used by Hooker in defence of the State Church, that the same persons constitute State and Church, and that therefore the government of both ought to rest in the same hands. This argument is invalid, while it is untrue; the members of the Church as a rule are members of the State, but millions of other members of the State are not members of the Church. While as far as the identity exists, it does not follow that the persons most fit to rule the State are also most fit to rule the Church. Take the case of a borough, whose inhabitants are all members of a local charity-organization: as a rule, its civil magistrates ought not to be the officers of its charity-organization.

public morality and order shall be done by her. But while the government of the State by State-powers is a godly institution, the government of the Church by the same officials, in opposition to the kingly dignity of Christ, is opposed to His will, and should be abolished.

To perceive more fully how strongly the connection of the Church with the State is opposed to the fundamental principles of God's kingdom, it is necessary to look more closely to the difference already observed, that the kingdom of God is spiritual in its origin and in the nature of its agencies, its laws, and its aims, while the State is of the earth, earthly.

This difference is indicated by Christ Himself in His celebrated words, spoken while standing before Pilate (John xviii. 36): "My kingdom is not of this world; if My kingdom were of this world, then would My servants fight, that I should not be delivered to the Jews, but now is My kingdom not from hence." It is clear that Christ in these words states—first, that His kingdom is of heavenly origin; secondly, that this origin determines the nature of its institutions; and, thirdly, that on this account it is entirely different from the kingdoms of this world; while the position of Christ when He spoke them—a poor, friendless man, condemned by His people as a blasphemer, on the point of dying on the Cross—is the most touching and powerful confirmation of the meaning of these words. But it is not less clear that in these words the principle of State-Churches is condemned in the most explicit manner, and that the upholders of the government over the Church by the kingdoms of this world act in direct opposition to the authority of Christ Himself, He having declared that the two do not agree together in their nature nor in the means which they use.

An objection is made against this argument, that the difference indicated by Christ, existed only between His kingdom and the kingdom of this world then existing, because these were heathenish, but not with regard to the present earthly kingdom of a Protestant nation. But the proof for the difference, given by Christ Himself, is taken not from the heathen-customs of His time, but from what is inherent in the nature of the earthly kingdoms of all times, that outward means are used in the defence of their kings, while the use of those means is opposed to the spiritual character of the kingdom of heaven.

And these words of Christ before Pilate stand not by themselves alone. The whole character of Christ's history is against the theory of the connection of the Church with the State. If Christ had thought that State-establishments were essential to the promotion of the prosperity of His Church, He would Himself have occupied an earthly throne at the head of a world-empire, more extensive and mightier than the throne of the Cæsars, or of any other king who ever ruled on earth. He would, in

His first advent, have occupied the position which, according to the Scriptures, He will occupy at His second coming. If He had chosen to do so, what could have hindered Him, the *Logos*, to direct the course of the world's history so that the offspring of David was at the time of His birth in possession of a world-dominion more powerful than that of Rome, and that He had found the way prepared to use all the resources which such a dominion would have placed at His disposition for the benefit of His Church in a degree which never by any other earthly power has been or can be reached, and without many of the drawbacks that are necessarily connected with the exercise of authority over the Church by short-sighted and imperfect earthly powers? But, instead of this, He was born while the house of David, in His mother, show its submission to the Roman dominion by being, on the command of Cæsar Augustus, at Bethlehem of Judea; in a cradle, among the workmen-class; later Himself a workman, poor among the poor to the extent that He lacked what the foxes and the birds of the air had—a place where to lay His head. The popular desire to make Him an earthly king, He frustrated not only by evading its fulfilment, but by destroying it through the setting forth of the spiritual character of His real dignity in the most unmistakable terms (John vi.). Nothing was done by Him to attract especially the higher classes to His kingdom. The men whom He chose to be the chief promoters of His kingdom on earth were mostly Galilean fishermen, none from among the higher classes of society.

The condition of society in which He chose to become man and to live was such, that nothing else than hostility against His influence could be expected from those in authority; and the unsparing force with which He rebuked the wickedness and attacked the prejudices of the high as well as the low, prepared the way to the Cross on which He died. That Cross, according to His Word, was the end for which He came in the world (Matt. xx. 28; John iii. 14–17; xii. 24); it is the fundamental basis on which the kingdom of heaven is built (1 Cor. i. 23, 24; ii. 2; iii. 11; 1 Peter ii. 4–8); the power through which He reigns over His Church (Rom. v. 21), and triumphs over His enemies (Heb. ii. 14; Col. ii. 14, 15); the emblem of the character of His Church (Matt. xvi. 24, 25; John xii. 24–26; xv. 20; Matt. xx. 25–28; Rom. vi. 5, 6; Gal. v. 24; vi. 14); and through all this the final plea that settles for ever the condemnation of the establishment of the Church, which stands in such relation to that Cross, by the kingdoms of this world.

Nor is the history of Christ's rule over His Church after His ascension to heaven more favourable to the principle of Church-establishments. How does He establish His Church on earth? Is it by using the power, which He has received by His enthronement on the right hand of His Father in heaven over the kingdoms and resources of the earth, to procure for the trembling, poor, in earthly things uninfluential handful of bewildered followers, which constituted the elements with which to form His Church at that time, the organizing authority, the mighty protection, the social prestige, the vast resources of one of the powers of the earth, which the Church, if ever, then would have needed for her establishment and her work in a hostile world? Is His first care to dispatch a delegation of His apostles to Cæsar Tiberius, on Rome's world-throne, with the humble request that it might please him to take Christianity under his protection, or with the charge to preach the Gospel with becoming reverence and dignity to him, while Christ Himself, appearing on the clouds of heaven in all the majesty of His glory, in the tone of authority which allows no denial, induces the mighty Emperor to cast away his idols, and to become the powerful protector of Christianity? Christ had the power to do it, but was this His course of action? Instead of this He establishes His Church by the Pentecostal effusion of the Holy Ghost (Acts ii.), that by His influence His followers may be united with Him in continual fellowship as the body is with the head, and in Him with one another, and may be able to establish Christianity in the world as a new spiritual dispensation of which Christ is the source, the life and the strength. And what does He do to enable them to knead the leaven of the kingdom of heaven in humanity? If ever necessary, then was it the time to aid the preaching of the Gospel by outward support, safe endowments and earthly protection, because His disciples were few in number, generally low in social station, small in worldly attainments, while the opposition was overwhelmingly large, nothing less than the whole world, with all its variety in its most mighty tendencies, in nothing one but in its enmity against Christ and His kingdom; the formalism and the fanaticism of the Jews, the superstition and the scepticism of the heathen, the infatuation and the prejudice of the philosophers, mingled everywhere with the moral depravity of one of the most degraded periods of the world's history. What does Christ do to help His chosen few to face all these mighty obstacles in the fulfilment of His commandment: "Go, make all the nations My disciples, baptizing them in the name of the Father and of the Son and of the Holy Ghost; teaching them to observe all things whatsoever I have commanded you" (Matt. xxviii. 19, 20)? Does He secure for them the goodwill, or at least the neutrality of those in authority? No; though having all power to control the mighty of the earth, He allows during the first three centuries, humanly spoken the most critical and the most trying in the whole history of Christianity, nearly without intermission, first the Jewish then the Roman authorities, from the Emperor down to the jailer, to manifest their continual hostility against Christianity and its propagation, with the fire of persecution always burning or smoking somewhere, but several times bursting out in the most intense fury all over the Roman Empire, devouring thousands upon thousands of the youthful Church in the most cruel manner; and He inscribes thereby in the Church history of the first three centuries in flaming letters for all future ages with His own hand the maxims for the establishment of His Church : " Verily, verily I say unto you, Except a corn of wheat fall into the ground and die it abideth alone; but if it die it bringeth forth much fruit." (John xii. 24). *Semen ecclesiæ est sanguis Christianorum*, "the blood of the Christians is the seed of the Church;" * and gives as ensign of the banner of His Church the token of the Cross, with the inscription *Hac vince*, " this is your triumph."

But how does He then enable His servants to do their holy work ? The Pentecostal blessing gives the answer. The whole history of the establishment of the kingdom of heaven in the world is a manifestation of the principle of the prophet, " Not by might, nor by power, but by My Spirit, saith the Lord of Hosts" (Zech. iv. 6). By His Spirit He emboldens the fallen Peter—who a few weeks ago had denied Him before a simple servant-maid—to stand in the temple before the thousands of Israel with the imposing message : " This Jesus, whom ye have crucified, hath God made both Lord and Christ;" and to add through one sermon about three thousand

* Tertull., "Apologet." *ad finem.*

souls to the Church of the Crucified (Acts ii. 36–41). By His Spirit He leads them into all truth, and causes the truth to go forth in the world in all its purity, extent, and force, commending itself to every man's conscience; convincing the world of sin, of righteousness, and of judgment; conquering prejudice, pride, enmity, carnality, and egoism; setting free the slaves of sin in the willing obedience to God and His will, and subduing the most inveterate errors and wickedness to its irresistible influence (John xvi. 7–15; Rom. i. 16; 2 Cor. iv. 2; John viii. 32). By His influence He gave the Stephens grace when dying to overcome the furious rage of their enemies by their indomitable boldness and meekness; the Polycarps to prove that love to their Lord and Saviour was stronger than the combined influence of indignities, flattery, suffering, and death; and the Blandinas with superhuman perseverance, while sustaining all the coarse and refined cruelties which unrestrained heathen hatred could invent, to exhort their fellow-sufferers to faithfulness, and to die themselves loyal to their heavenly King. By His Spirit He opened the hearts of the Lydias to attend to what was spoken of the Pauls; and gave increase to the Word, wherever it was planted and watered, with the result that after three centuries of labour, struggle, and suffering He had made Christianity supersede heathenism as the most influential religion in the world, against all the resources of earthly powers, and thereby had established it beyond doubt for all following ages, that according to the will of Christ His Church has to stand and to conquer in the world on its own merits and by the power of His Spirit.

And the reason for this spiritual character of the means used by Christ for the establishment of His Church on the earth we find in the very purpose of the kingdom of heaven itself. That purpose is to save sinners from their sins (Matt. i. 21; Luke xix. 10). That sin is, that humanity is fallen away from God, and has become κόσμος, *world*—that is, that no longer God but the world, and self as part of the world, is the centre of his life; for the world, sinful humanity lives; the delights of the world it seeks; the impulses inspired by the world it follows; on the resources of the world it endeavours to lean. Christ consequently came to bring man back from allegiance to the world to allegiance to God (John i. 10-12; 1 John ii. 15-17; John iii. 16-21; xiv. 6). His purpose, therefore, demands that Christ uses the means adapted to deliver man from his sinful allegiance to the world, and to re-establish the life of God in his heart—that is, while God is Spirit, He must use spiritual influences which can make man a new creature, living and walking by the Spirit, to give God the place which hitherto the world has occupied in his life.

But the employment of earthly power, earthly riches, earthly prestige, earthly honour for the promotion of the coming of His kingdom, could only strengthen the very allegiance to the world which He came to destroy. His whole influence, therefore, tends to break the spell wherewith these earthly influences keep the hearts of men bound, and hinder the coming of His kingdom in them. So deeply is this tendency interwoven with the history of the establishment of His kingdom on earth, that He deemed even His bodily presence on earth an hindrance, which was to be removed before that establishment could be achieved by the coming of the Spirit (John xvi. 7–11; conf. 2 Cor. v. 16).

Surely Christ has no sympathy with the narrow and morose contempt of the world which many take as the very essence of Christianity. He who, as the *Logos*, has created the world, with all its beauties, richness, and delights; who, on the marriage feast at Cana, made the water wine; who wept at the grave of Lazarus, and nourished friendship for John and filial love for His mother, even on the Cross, cannot be pleased with contempt of the world. But what He intends is, to bring men to the unreserved surrender of the heart to God and His will, by counting all things loss for the excellency of the knowledge of Christ (Philip. iii. 7–11), that Christ might be gained, and in Him as much of earthly resources as God is pleased to give; and to achieve this purpose it is His will that those earthly influences which tend to strengthen the worldliness of the sinner's heart, be not mixed up with the spiritual means appointed by Him to promote the coming of His kingdom in the world.

The establishment of the Church by the State being a fruitful source of mingling earthly influences with the ordinances of the Gospel for the promotion of the coming of God's kingdom in the world, is therefore opposed to the very essence of Christianity, and as such most earnestly to be avoided.

The same spiritual character of the kingdom of heaven causes it to be incongruous that the Church should be subjected to the leading characteristics necessarily connected with the government of every earthly State.

The kingdom of heaven, in consequence of its spiritual principle, attaches paramount value to, and seeks to influence accordingly, the condition of the heart. Outward worship, without the worship of the heart, is rejected as not pleasing to the Most Holy (John iv. 23, 24; Matt. xv. 7-9; xxiii. 23-28). The largest gifts to the poor, done to be seen by men, are condemned as guilty show (Matt. vi. 1-4; 1 Cor. xiii. 3). Converted harlots and publicans are set above the most zealous Pharisees (Matt. xxi. 31, 32; Luke vii. 36-47). One of the first principles of good Church-rule, therefore, is assiduously to counteract the self-deceit fostered by outward heartless worship and works, and to direct all its influence to the production and promotion of that renewal of the spirit of the mind which constitutes the new man, "created after God in righteousness and true holiness" (Eph. iv. 20–24). Truth in the inner man, not uniformity in the outward demeanour, is its chief aim. The object of the rule of the State, on the contrary, is the outward demeanour. The modern notions of a free, well-organized State tend to confine its sphere to the public life; to guarantee as far as possible the freedom of private life from all interference by State-influences and to brand all unlawful State-influences even as a crime. Consequently, it is England's boast that its laws and justice regard only acts and words, not thoughts and feelings; that one of its professed State-principles is, to respect even the privacy of individual homes. And its State acknowledges as good citizens those who promote public order and well-being. The consequence is, that the State, undertaking to rule the Church, applies in her Church-rule the same principle; dictates to the Church, by her outward authority, what she has to believe, without regard to the conviction of the heart, which alone can constitute faith in a truly Christian sense; regulates, on the ground of political considerations and traditions, the outward form of worship and government, and imposes on her an outward uniformity in practices and words in violation of the principle of the Spirit, who, to promote the only worship and Church life which is acceptable to God, that in spirit and in truth, commands and works inward union of the heart in faith, hope, and love, with entire freedom of the different individualities to manifest the devotion of their heart and to regulate their Church-form under the influence of the Spirit, within the limits of the dictates of God's Word, in the forms most suitable to their individual conscience.

Closely connected with this is the still more fundamental difference, that grace rules in the Church and law in the State. This is not to be understood in the sense that law should not be honoured in the Church. In the Church, as well as in the State, its authority, its obligatory force, the duty of obeying it, and the necessity of the punishment of its violation, is acknowledged; and if there is in this respect any difference between the two, the Church having to do with the perfect law of the most holy God, unmixed with human errors, arbitrariness, or unrighteousness, ought certainly to be the staunchest upholder of the law's majesty. The unequivocal language of her Head (Matt. v. 17-20) points in that direction, and one of her chief members, the Apostle Paul, speaks in her name: "Do we then make void the law through faith? God forbid; we establish the law" (Rom. iii. 31). But the means used in both to produce the fulfilment of the law, and to vindicate its majesty, are entirely different. Both acknowledge that the violated majesty of the law must be vindicated, in order that the authority of the law might not be weakened and the observance of the law might be promoted. But the State, assuming that nothing prevents the fulfilment of its laws by any well-disposed citizen, and determined that its violation shall be repressed, and thereby the decay of the respect due to it shall be prevented, entrusts that vindication to the law itself and its organs, whose duty it is, wherever a violation of the law is officially brought and proved before them in the manner by the law ordained, to apply the penalties by the law prescribed, with that sternness which subjects all other considerations to the upholding of the authority of the law, which is the guardian and the guarantee of the coherence, order, and well-being of the commonwealth. The winking at any violation of the majesty of the law is deemed to be worse than the lawlessness of the lawless classes in weakening the respect for the law, without which the State cannot prosper. The Church, on the contrary, deeply conscious that all flesh hath sinned, that is, lives in lawlessness (ἀνομία, 1 John iii. 4), in enmity against the law, that therefore the law has become the strength of sin, an incitation to more sin (Rom. viii. 7; vii. 8–14; 1 Cor. xv. 56), and that no flesh shall be justified by the deeds of the law, because by the law is the knowledge of sin (Rom. iii. 19, 20), glories in the Gospel, that with respect to her manifold and great sins, the majesty of God's law is honoured, its holiness vindicated, its demands satisfied through the infinite mercy of God in the person of her Head, who being above the law, was "made under the law to redeem His Church from the curse of the law, being made a curse for her" (Gal. iv. 4; iii. 13); who being without sin Himself, was, in consequence of His having become man, made sin for His Church, that she might be made the righteousness of God in Him (2 Cor. v. 21); and who by the perfect obedience which He has learned by the things which He suffered, makes righteous all who are united to Him by a living faith (Rom. v. 19; Heb. v. 8, 9). God, whose law she had offended, has in His infinite mercy His own Son prepared to be a propitiation for her violation of the law, that He might be just and the justifier of all who believe in Jesus (Rom. iii. 25). In Christ, God Himself comes reconciling to the hearts of sinful men, who deserve the full experience of the curse of the law, with the fulness of His favour by the Holy Spirit, to conquer their enmity, to make them love Him, and in that love to bring them to the hearty obedience of the law, which consists in the love of God and His commandments. By that grace He continues to rule the Church; stirs up, entertains, strengthens, deepens her willing observance of His law, and leads her to find more and more in the fulfilment of that law, the fruition of life eternal. How is it possible that the Church, which finds the vindication of the violated law in Christ's sacrifice and the power to bring to and to keep in the observance of the law, in God's grace in Christ, can be properly ruled according to the principles of the State, which seeks both in the ordinances of the law itself?

In consequence of this difference, repentance finds in the State but a very secondary place. It may in some cases be acknowledged as a partial vindication of the majesty of the violated law, and as such induce and justify the judge to inflict a minor punishment; but it would be a subversion of all social order, if a thief, a robber, a murderer should be left unpunished if he repented, even should his repentance in all respects prove to be honest and deep. To let the repentant culprit free would be deemed unfaithful and unjust, destroying all respect for the law, in proportion to the greatness of the guilt. So little place finds repentance in the State, that it restrains rather than induces the accused to confess their guilt and exempt them from the obligation to accuse themselves. In the Church, on the contrary, the golden rule is: "If we confess our sins, God is faithful and just to forgive us our sins and to cleanse us from all unrighteousness" (1 John i. 9). The publican is declared justified on the earnest prayer, "God be merciful to me a sinner" (Luke xviii. 10-14). Criminals dying the felon's death according to their own confession justly, on their simple request, "Lord, remember me when Thou comest into Thy kingdom," receive the assurance that they shall be at once admitted to the presence of the Divine

King in paradise (Luke xxiii. 40–43). All Christ's dealings with His Church are directed to produce, to strengthen, to deepen repentance in the sinner's heart; through the law to give the knowledge of sin and of its curse (Rom. iii. 20; Gal. ii. 19); through the gospel to make the stony heart flesh and the stubborn heart submissive; while full forgiveness, unreserved acceptance in God's fatherly favour, streams of eternal life are ready to burst over the heart that in true repentance turns to God, no matter how great the sins have been with which it is polluted. So deeply interwoven is this with the essence of the Church, that the Apostle Paul dares to say, "Where sin has abounded, grace has much more abounded" (Rom. v. 20), and that Christ Himself sets the measure of forgiveness as the measure of love, which is the fulfilment of the law (Luke vii. 47). While, therefore, with the State in its relation to the law-breakers unbending sternness in the maintenance of the law prevails, and should prevail, ought the relation of the Church to the guilty, even in her discipline, to be characterized by unconquerable pity and love. How is it possible that the Church can be ruled properly, according to the principles of the State?

Another manifestation of the same fundamental difference is, that in the State the principle rules: "An eye for an eye, and a tooth for a tooth;" therefore, that offenders must be punished according to their deserts. Every one who permits a thief, a robber, a murderer, by whom he has suffered, to be free from the arm of justice, even if it were from the noblest of motives, would be guilty of loosening the authority of the law and the fundamentals of social order. In the Church, on the contrary, the Kingly rule is: "Love your enemies, bless them that curse you, do good to them that hate you, and pray for them which despitefully use you and persecute you; that ye may be the children of your Father which is in heaven; for He maketh His sun to rise on the evil and on the good, and sendeth rain on the just and on the unjust" (Matt. v. 44, 45). Being herself much forgiven, and through first love brought to obedience to the law, it is her duty, and, as far as grace has triumphed, her delight, to make her enemies feel in her own love something of the holy love of God, that seeks to conquer their enmity by forgiving their offences and even by leaving them unpunished, as far as her duties toward others allow it. How is it possible that the Church can be properly ruled according to the principles of the State?

A third difference, resulting from the opposite nature of the Church and the State, is what Christ Himself pressed before Pilate as a proof that His kingdom was not of this world; namely, that the State uses, and is justified in using, outward means to enforce its laws and defend its rights. Fines, imprisonment, death even, if necessary, are the penalties which it inflicts where its laws are violated. It puts the truncheon, the sword and the gun in the hands of its police, its army and navy, to overcome the enemies of its well-being within and without its pale. Having outward earthly interests to promote amidst outward earthly influences, it is bound to be able to act upon them by earthly means. The Church's interests, on the contrary, being exclusively spiritual, she relies on spiritual means alone to make her institutions observed and her rights respected. " The weapons of her warfare are not carnal, but mighty through God to the pulling down of strongholds" (2 Cor. x. 4); the " girdle of her loins is truth; her breastplate righteousness; her sandals the preparation of the gospel of peace; her shield faith; her helmet salvation; her sword the Word of God" (Eph. vi. 14-17). Her heavenly Lord Himself is her defence; His Spirit her power; His dominion her safety. Every use of outward force in her defence is alien from, and therefore vitiating, her spiritual character. Even her discipline she has to exercise by means of advice, private rebuke, open censure, prohibition of the use of the Lord's Supper, excommunication from her fellowship, with the repentance of the guilty and the vindication of the integrity of the body of Christ for her aim, and under the decisive influence of the Holy Ghost.

There can be no doubt, after looking on the difference which exists between the nature of the Church and the State, that the subjection of the Church to the legislative, administrative, and judicial power of the State is against the fundamental principles of Christ's kingdom. This becomes still more apparent, if we direct our attention particularly to some of the chief evils which are the necessary results of this incongruous connection.

We have already indicated how unseemly it is that the men who rule the State, should at the same time rule the Church. But the importance of this fact demands somewhat closer attention. It may be taken as a general rule that an institution can only be properly ruled by agencies who understand and identify themselves with its character, its vocation and its demands. According to this rule, it is impossible that the government over two institutions so entirely differing from one another as Church and State can properly rest in the hands of the same men. The requirements for the proper government of each of them are so large, and so essentially different from each other, that the same men cannot be supposed to possess them. Different kind of men, different habits of mind and life, different studies, each of such extent that they require a lifetime, different practical tact are wanted for both. For the proper government of the State are wanted shrewd, businesslike worldmen (*weltmänner*), of commanding temper, versed in the knowledge of the different institutions of the people and their manner of working; of the different laws, both in their excellency and in their defects; with a quick eye to discern the real interests and the actual wishes of the people, together with the best moment and the best form to promote them in a manner satisfying alike to the demands of justice and of the historical traditions and the present tendencies of the people ; eager to get all the light that the history of their country and their times, the experience of former ages and of their contemporaries, the best statistics, and the different branches of social and political sciences can give to aid them in the promotion of the prosperity and influence of the State, and able to control the chaos of conflicting interests of opposite social powers and individualities sufficiently to unite them in devising, forming, and properly executing measures that will prove practicable and beneficial.

For the proper government of the Church, on the contrary, are wanted pious, holy men of God, full of the Holy Ghost, glowing with unconquerable love, whose conversation is in heaven, depending on heavenly influences for wisdom, power, and success, prepared by knowledge of their own heart and of the working of God's grace within them, to enter with a sympathising heart into the wants and wishes of their people, to bring and to keep them in living fellowship with Christ and His kingdom ; aiming to get at the truth as it is in Jesus by all the means which Biblical criticism and exegesis, Church-history and dogmatics afford ; seeking to edify their people in love, both by their work and their example, and to promote among them all that is true, and honest, and just, and pure, and lovely, and of good report.

The consequence is, that whenever the State-authorities have to exercise the government of the Church, they find themselves called to the fulfilment of a task of the highest importance without the possession of the necessary requirements, which cannot be otherwise than an immoral position for themselves and a great injury to the Church. The inevitable result is, that the principles of State-government are applied to the government of the Church by which the spiritual independence of the Church is paralyzed by the State's official formality; the warm glow of grace's dominion in the Church chilled by the law habits of the State; the Spirit's influence over the Church in her worship and discipline quenched by State-precepts and customs, and in general on the true Church-life inflicted the injury (even allowed the best case, that the Church does not change her own principles for the principles of the State's life) of forcing her in a garment not fit for her use. To understand the full absurdity of the exercise of Church-government by the State, it is only necessary to realize the actual state of things by a telling example. Legislative power over the ritual, doctrine, discipline, and government of the Episcopal Church in England rests in both Houses of Parliament. On the whole, they command and deserve the respect of the world as the best legislative assembly for constitutional spirit that the world can show. Without doubt, there are not a few true Christians among them. But, with the exception of

AN APPEAL TO THE CONSCIENCE. 41

a few occupants of the Episcopal bench in the House of Lords, and a few champions of religious parties or of Protestantism, with some extra knowledge of their specialities, none are endowed with the special capacities necessary to make good Church-laws. The members of the House of Commons are chosen for their eminence in statesmanship, for their general political or social influence, or as representing some special interest; for their eloquence and business-tact; for their party-bias on ecclesiastical questions, while social integrity and respectability as a rule, are good recommendations to popularity; but not for the essential qualities of a good Church-ruler. The members of the House of Lords are constituted lawgivers to the Church mainly in consequence of their being heirs by birth of influential titles; nor are they educated with a view to enable them to discharge their duties as lawgivers of the Church. The consequence is, that the deliberations in both Houses of Parliament on Church-questions rest on the same principles of statesmanship, expediency, and justice as those over State-affairs; but that discussions affecting the deepest life of the Church, the life of the Spirit, upon the true meaning of the doctrine of the New Testament, in some fundamental question of Christian truth, worship, discipline or Church government, are not undertaken, and are felt to be out of place in Parliament. Even the best qualified and best disposed members deliberate in

Parliament on Church matters as a special part of State-interests. The Church, as a Church, is unrepresented, even in name, except by a few of her officers; while she is subjected to the indignity of being obliged to acknowledge the legal right to decide on her dearest interests, to belong to a considerable number of her deadliest enemies; to Roman Catholics to vote on questions affecting her Protestant character; to Jews to vote on the value of the Cross and the divine glory of her Head; to infidels to vote on the influence of the Spirit of God and the means to promote it; and to slaves of their passions and lusts to vote on her discipline and worship.

The same indignity, only on a more extensive scale, is inflicted on the Church by submitting her as a State-institution to the control of the nation at large, and to the voting influence of all classes of people, even of the most degraded and the most hostile to her prosperity and existence.

This state of affairs, inherent in the character of a State-establishment, makes it the imperative duty of every true friend of the Church to exert his best endeavours to remove such pernicious influences from the blood-bought body of Christ and from the spiritual temple of God.

Another influential evil, necessarily following from the connection of the Church with the State, is that it destroys the Church as a Church in the sense of Christ and His apostles. Even the word with which she is named in the New Testament (ἐκκλησία) indicates that it is essential to her character to be *called out of the world* —therefore separated from the world, not indeed living in a separate dwelling-place, but in her religious and moral life (John xvii. 15), and that as the names usually given to her (Kingdom of Heaven, Body of Christ, House of God, True Vine, Flock of the Good Shepherd), and the description of her existence and working (Matt. xiii. ; Eph. i. 22, 23 ; ii. 19-22 ; iv. 1-16 ; 1 Cor. xii. 12-31 ; 1 Peter ii. 1-10 ; John x., xv., xvii.) show, by being not a loosely-connected aggregate of men, united only by the Christian name and a few religious ordinances, but a living religious and moral organization, the condition of whose existence, the character and spring of whose life is fellowship by faith with Christ in the Holy Ghost; whose visible form, in the midst of the world, is characterized by the outward manifestations of that inward fellowship with the Redeemer in the confession, the worship, and the service of Christ, according to His Word, under a government adapted to its nature. Those who share by faith her fellowship with Christ are her true members, the kernel of her organism, necessary for the preservation of her character—as it were, her soul, in which resides her self-consciousness, the principle of her life and growth, and through which she is the temple of the Holy Ghost. To the Church, as a body, belong all who, acceptably to her, profess to partake in her confession, worship, and service of Christ, which, through her impossibility to discern the hearts of the professors, of necessity includes many who are not in living fellowship with Christ, and therefore not really members of His body, though these incongruous elements, where kept under control of the true Church life by discipline and the power of the Spirit, are not able to destroy the healthy condition of the body of believers. The true Church, living by faith in fellowship with Christ, is one, because Christ is one, though its outward manifestation, by reason of its being influenced by different individualities, traditions, circumstances of life and time, and nationalities of her members, shows itself in the different denominational Church organizations, who possess in various degrees the necessary qualities of the true Church. But through her connection with the State the organization which characterizes the Church as a body, separate from the world, is broken. The vital principle of her organism—to acknowledge Christ as her Head, by regulating her spiritual life solely in accordance with His will, is weakened; she has to look to the State to know what she has to believe, and how she has to worship her heavenly King. She includes not only those who voluntarily profess to join her in her worship and her service of Christ, but, according to her ideal as a State-Church, the whole nation is parcelled out to her in a closely-fitting set of parishes; and, in reality, while her connection with the State has virtually paralyzed her discipline, which is the guardian of her purity and vitality, a large part join her for the sake of the social advantages which belong to a State-Church, but who do not care for her confession or her worship. The consequence is, that she has become a State-institution for the worship and the promotion of religious influences among the people, called by the name of Church, but which has lost the essential characteristics of the Church of Christ and the apostles; while in her the most heterogeneous elements of truth and error; of Evangelicals, Romanists, and Rationalists; of true church, and false church, and no-church; of piety, superstition, infidelity, worldliness and indifference—not secretly and under control of the true Church-spirit, as in every other visible Church, but professedly and unrestrained—are united, not by the vital principle of a true Church-organization, faith in Christ, and the influence of the Holy Ghost, but by a form of worship and of government regulated and imposed by law; by a hierarchy, organized, endowed, and in a large measure nominated, by the State, and by the infatuation which social advantage, resulting from her connection with the State, and the antiquity of that connection, engender. So far has the connection with the State suppressed all true Church-life in the State-Church, that even her best members have lost to a large degree the consciousness of her degeneracy by her connection with the State, and deem that connection her rock of safety and her glory. All sorts of Church-theories are invented by the defenders of that connection in order to try to get one that will suit the existing state of affairs, and, consequently, will make the cherished State-connection seem consistent with her name of *Church*, though sacrificing her true Church-character.

Not less false is the position to which the State-connection of the Church reduces the State. That connection invests the State, as already shown, with the duty of Church-government, for which she is not fit; a position in every respect intolerable for men who feel their responsibility, but especially indefensible where the interests of religion are concerned and, as at the present time, are intensely stirred by the fierce contest over the fundamental principles of Christianity on questions of its historical facts, doctrine, Church-government and worship. None but men fitly endowed ought to stand at the helm of the Church in the midst of the storm. But the position of the State in her relation to the State-Church is still more anomalous by reason of her duty to all who do not belong to her communion. There are millions of religiously disposed people in this kingdom who have Church-organizations of their own. Still they belong to the State. The government of the State is bound by the principles of justice and equity to promote their interests equally with those of State-Churchmen; but by her connection with the State-Church the State ensures to that one Church a large amount of financial, political and social advantages, and causes thereby to the same extent to the other half of the nation corresponding disadvantage; as with a balance, weights placed on one side exercise a corresponding opposite influence on the other. But one of the chief duties of the State is to exercise equal justice to all. At the same time, she entertains in that way throughout the whole nation a spirit of haughtiness on the one side, of discontent and animosity on the other; on all sides, of discord and strife dividing English society into two hostile camps, engaged continually in more or less active warfare. Now, this is a state of things which seriously interferes with the true interests and the happiness of the people; it engenders a continual social fever which seriously injures the national life, and lays on her the guilt of hindering the national interests which it is her duty to promote.

How can a Church, acknowledging her allegiance to Christ, with a good conscience allow, for the sake of earthly advantages, such a state of things to continue, which makes her, called to be an unmixed instrumentality of moral health and peace, in one respect a continual source of irritation and disease in the national body, and a stain on the excellency of the English Constitution?

Another evil consequence of the connection of the

Church with the State is the manner in which the clergy too often obtain their different charges. The most commendable mode of election to a position whose blessing depends in such a large measure upon the confidence with regard to the deepest and most delicate interests of the heart and life which exists between the clergy and their people, seems to be that of which we find an example in the New Testament (Acts vi.) in the election of the first deacons, and which prevailed in a large degree within the Church of the first centuries,* that the people shall choose their own pastors from duly qualified persons. Now in the State-Church of England, in the great majority of cases, the members of the Church possess no influence in the election of their clergy, whether of higher or lower degree. The archbishops, bishops, and other dignitaries are virtually elected by the State; a great number of Church-livings are at the disposal of the Lord Chancellor and other State-officers; still more under some peer or squire perhaps in no connection with, or even in hostility against the Church and her ordinances, without any guarantee that the true spiritual interests of the people shall be the leading motive of the election. The consequence is, the disgraceful sale of Church-livings at public auction to the highest bidder; the offering for sale of Church-livings to be constantly seen among the

---

* Conf. Bingham: "Antiquities of the Christian Church," iv. c. 2.

advertisements in newspapers; and well-known agencies are allowed to effect the transfer of Church-livings for a certain sum of money, a habit utterly alien from, and particularly offensive to the sentiment of all other Protestant Churches, for which perhaps only some parallel can be found in the most degraded times of the Roman Catholic Church, though England in the Middle Ages did know how to oppose it,* but which is openly suffered to continue year after year in the Episcopal Church in England in this enlightened nineteenth century. This state of things is the fruit of her connection with the State. Left to herself, the right of nomination by State-officials would, of course, devolve upon her; while the disgraceful practice of the disposing of Church-livings by sale, and even the nomination by civil patrons could not endure, were the true Church-life aroused from the stupor which is caused by her connection with the State.

Nor are the reasons, commonly derived from the principles of the kingdom of heaven, in defence of the connection of the Church with the State, of any avail.

One of these is, that a State-connection counteracts the priestly dominion over the Church by leaving the main power over her affairs in lay-hands. But a strong *primâ facie* case against this argument is made out by the fact, that in no

* Conf. the "Inhibitions of Stephanus and Richardus apud Gibson," l. l. p. 797.

Protestant Church-denomination in England is the question of priestly dominion apparent but in its State-Church. All other denominations, being sturdy adherents of the Protestant principle of the priesthood of all believers, leave no place for a separate priesthood, one of the corruptions of the Romish leaven, under cover of the State allowed to remain in the State-Church of England; while there is no complaint about undue influence exercised by the ministry in any of these bodies. And a little reflection makes it clear that this statement is fully confirmed by the real facts of the case. The overbearing priestly pretensions are nothing else but the worldly passion for power and dominion, seeking gratification in the ecclesiastical sphere. Now this evil finds a more congenial soil in a church endowed with the prestige and social ascendency of State-authority than in the humbler and purer ground of churches depending only upon the influences of the Spirit. Besides the lay-influences, which alone can be a real blessing for the Church, those of holy members of the Church, living through the Spirit, belong of necessity in proportion more to the churches depending only upon spiritual influences than to the State-Church; while what are called the lay-influences, exercised by the State, do not deserve that name, because many persons from whom they emanate, though not belonging to the priesthood, stand in no personal relation to the Church over which they exercise authority; while the name laity, whenever there is a question of ecclesiastical affairs in distinction from the priesthood, can only be properly applied to those who belong to the flock of the Church.*

Of no more value is the argument, that the State-connection promotes the catholicity of the Church. On the contrary, as the Spirit of Christ knows no limits but the truth and the will of God; as His range is therefore much wider than that of the State, may the churches which are ruled by the influences of the Spirit, be expected to be more truly large-hearted than the Church ruled by the State. The latter becomes, at least in a certain sense, a national church, identifying itself with the peculiarities, animosities and pride which the nation fosters against the other nations of the earth; while for the first, under the influence of the Spirit, no limits of nationality or country exist. In Christ there is neither Greek nor Jew, neither Barbarian nor Scythian, but Christ is all in all.

* The word λαϊκός seems to have originated in Jewish Hellenistic circles. It is first found by Aquila, Symmachus and Theodotion, ad 1 Sam. xxi. 4, 5, and by Symmachus and Theodotion, ad Ezek. xlviii. 15, in opposition to the Jewish priests and Levites. Very soon it found ready entrance in the Christian Church, to designate the Church flock in distinction from the Church-officers. (Conf. " Clem. Rom. Ep. ad Corinth.," c. 40, and Jacobson, ad h.l.; Cornelius, " Ep. ad Fabium apud Routh, Reliq. Sacr.," iii. pp. 21, 23, 26; Tertull., " De Præscriptionibus," c. 41; " De Fuga in Persec." c. 11; Hieron., " Ad Ezechielem," ed. Marian. Vict., tom. iv. p. 493; " Decretum Gratiani," part i. Dist. xxxiii. c. 6, etc. etc.; conf. etiam " Suiceri Thes. Eccles. sub voce "). The more general applications of the word seem to be derived from the original indicated sense.

Besides the uniformity of worship imposed on the State-Church by the State, is a wall of partition dividing her from those who do not conform to it, which for the churches dependent only upon the influences of the Spirit, does not exist; while the social ascendency which State-connection imparts is an impediment rather than a help for the full development of that pure love which, loving in Christ, embraces all whom Christ loves, and is thereby the only source of genuine Christian catholicity. The inclusiveness of which the State-Church boasts, is proved by the actual condition of the State-Church, to possess nothing in common with the catholicity which is the characteristic and the glory of Christ's Church. It is nothing else but the result from the outward bond, with which the advantages, flowing from the connection with the State, keep together Evangelicals, Romanists, and Rationalists, who differ in the most essential truths of Christianity, whose main relation towards one another is, besides some similarity in the form of worship with great difficulty maintained, their connection with the State and their acknowledgment of Episcopal authority. Outwardly bound together, they are more bitterly divided than any other three of the Protestant denominations in Great Britain. Instead of being a help of true Christian catholicity, this inclusiveness, artificially holding together elements which cannot coalesce, is a fruitful source of heartburning, envy, strife, and even law-suits; and while destroying the spiritual organization of the Church, degrades her to a battle-field of evil passions and an arena for intrigues.

A very common argument for the maintenance of the connection of the Church with the State is, that by it a focus of civilization is preserved for the benefit of many country-parishes, in the person and the family of the clergyman. Now, there can be no question that in many country-parishes the clergyman of the Church of England exercises a most beneficial civilizing influence, but that fact stands in no vital relation to the State-connection of the Episcopal Church, but depends more on the personal qualities of the clergy themselves. The same influence is apparent in the Dutch Reformed Church in the Netherlands, by reason of the rule of the Church demanding official proofs from every candidate to the holy ministry, of having taken in one of the universities of the country, a degree in mathematics, in classics and in theology, before admitting them to the final thorough examination by the Church-authorities; yet that Church is completely free from State-interference in her government and worship. Let only the position be called up before the mind, in which these country-parishes will be when the Church of England is disestablished, and it becomes at once clear that this advantage is not the fruit of the Church's connection with the State. It would be an insult to the beneficence and resources of the members of the

Church of England to suppose for a moment that even in those parishes which, through disestablishment, will lose their endowments for the maintenance of the clergy, disestablishment will cause the extinction of the agencies of the Church of England. As a rule, disestablishment will not deprive them of the presence of the clergy and their families. Neither will disestablishment lower the culture-standard of the clergy. That standard depends on university-education, and not on State-influences. The Episcopal Church, freed from State-supremacy, will certainly require of her clergy proofs of university-education as a condition of admission to her sacred ministry, and thereby maintain the culture of her clergy at the same level on which it stands at present; while their theological training will, doubtless, eventually be materially advanced; and therefore the cultivating influences of the clergy will not be destroyed by disestablishment. On the contrary, disestablishment will increase them. True cultivation exists in elevating all that is truly human in man. Now, the prestige with which the State-connection surrounds the established clergy, has the effect in not a few cases of introducing a tone of lofty condescension and of imperiousness in the clergyman's intercourse with his parishioners, which wounds true manhood to the quick; in other cases, entirely against the intention of the clergyman, the humbler parishioners are either overawed, or led to adopt a creeping servility, both tending to debase rather than raise the character of the parishioners. Disestablishment will remove from the clergy the hindrances to their partaking more fully in the deepest and purest cultivating influences which ever have been exercised on earth— those of the Lord Jesus Himself, seeking in a purely spiritual way to raise humanity to the highest possible culture in filial fellowship in Himself with God.

It stands, therefore, proved that the connection of the Church with the State is against the fundamental principles of the kingdom of heaven and, as such, against the will of Christ.

II.

That connection is against the will of Christ also, because it counteracts the working of God's Spirit in the hearts of believers of the Episcopal Church. Before, however, entering on this part of the argument, it is necessary to point out that it is not intended for a moment to deny the excellency of the piety of many members of the established Church. The Cranmers, Latimers, Ridleys; the Fletchers, Newtons, Cowpers; the Hannah Mores, Wilberforces, and a great many more, would be unanswerable proofs of the deep, practical, powerful piety which can be and is connected with the State-Church. But what is meant is, that the piety to be found in the State-Church is there in spite of the State-connection;

that even in the best instances the evil influences of this connection had to be conquered, while in several, even of the best instances, is to be traced what, from the nature of the case, must be deemed the normal influence of the State-connection, on the inner life of believing Church-members.

An actual proof of the evil tendency of the State-connection on the individual piety is to be found in the history of the English Reformation. What must strike everyone who reads that history, is that so many of its best and representative men, who ended by gloriously maintaining the principles of the Reformation, have either formally denied them, or, at least, more or less ambiguously maintained them on some former occasion. The formal denial of Cranmer and Bilney is remembered by all; but even from brave Latimer an uncertain sound occasionally issues, which indicates a sacrifice of his plain duty to State-influences.* Compare this fact with the history of the Reformation in the Netherlands, and we find among the thousands of those who died for their faith, scarcely any of the leading men hesitating in confessing their faith in the hour of trial. The hesitancy in several of the English reformers stands in mournful contrast to the single-hearted decision shown there, which evidently rejoices in the opportunity of testifying for what is their heart's life. Now, this difference, I think, finds its ex-

* Conf. Demaus, "Life of Latimer," pp. 139, 335.

planation in the State-connection of the English Church. In consequence of that connection, the English Reformation was but a half-hearted measure, depending upon the will of Henry VIII. as well as on a conscientious obedience to the truth. Besides, in consequence of the connection of the Church with the State, worldly considerations were, in a large measure, mingled with, though disguised by, the interests of religion, without consciousness in the usual course of events, even in the hearts of its best men. This mixture of motives in the hour of their trial became a snare to them, as well as their disgrace, though the principle of piety was proved sound afterwards, in many instances, by moving them to retract their denial, and to end as faithful witnesses of the truth. And that this is really a result, in the normal course of events, to be expected, will appear when we look somewhat more closely on the effect of union with the State upon the inward life of Churchmembers.

As already stated, the true characteristic of sin is, that man is fallen from God, and has given to the world (world including self) the place in his heart and life which belongs to God; the tendency of all Christ's saving influences, consequently, is to set man's heart free from the dominion of the world and to lead him back to God; while the connection of the Church with the State, mixing up worldly influences with the influences of Christianity, counteracts thereby the saving influence of the Spirit of Christ.

An application of this general principle to the particularities of the inner life will show its force.

One of the most powerful inborn tendencies of fallen humanity is to trust in, and to seek help from creature-influences rather than from the living God. So strong is this tendency, as constant experience teaches, that man as a rule does not actually commit himself and his interests into the hands of God, unless inwardly pressed by the utter deficiency of all creature-influences. Even the true believer has again and again, in the greater and smaller emergencies of his life, to be brought by the pressure of necessity to the actual committal of himself into the hands of his Father in heaven. The tendency of God's Spirit, on the contrary, is expressed in the solemn words: " Thus saith the Lord : Cursed be the man that trusteth in man, and maketh flesh his arm, and whose heart departeth from the Lord ; for he shall be like the heath in the desert, and shall not see when good cometh ; but shall inhabit the parched places in the wilderness, in a salt land and not inhabited. Blessed is the man that trusteth in the Lord, and whose hope the Lord is ; for he shall be as a tree planted by the waters, and that spreadeth out her roots by the river, and shall not see when heat cometh, but her leaf shall be green ; and shall not be careful in the year of drought, neither shall cease from yielding fruit" (Jerem. xvii.

5-8). No duty is more constantly and forcibly commanded both in the Old and New Testament. Everywhere it is inculcated as the very soul of true piety, and as the secret of the spiritual life of the Bible saints. And on what side is now the influence of the connection of the Church with the State? Is it a help with respect to the interests of the Church to bring to, and to keep men in unreserved confidence in God, or to the godless tendency of the sinful human heart to trust in creature-influences? Undoubtedly the latter. State-endowments are relied on for the maintenance of religious ordinances; State-influence for the power, the defence, and the prosperity of the Church; State-nominations, State-votes, and State-judges for the purity and maintenance of the confession of the truth. Surely there are noble examples of deep dependence upon God recorded on the Church's registers, but these exist not in consequence, but in spite of the connection with the State, by which they were tempted to take hold of that instead of God. So strongly is the State-connection paralyzing the actual confidence in God, with regard to the interests of the Church in the hearts of Churchmen, that not a few of the best of them continually exhibit unmistakable signs of a decided panic when the subject of disestablishment is advanced, as if the existence or the influence, or at least the prosperity of the Church herself could not survive the breaking of her bonds with the State.

Another tendency of the sinful human heart is the desire to be the first in the estimation of men, frequently combined with passion for influence and dominion, not for the sake of the good that can be done, but for the satisfaction which the exercise of it gives to the pride of the heart. There is no tendency which Christ more earnestly rebuked, even in His disciples. So He answered the question of His apostles: " Who is the greatest in the kingdom of heaven?" by setting a little child in the midst of them, and uttering the solemn warning: " Verily I say unto you, Except ye be converted and become as little children, ye shall not enter into the kingdom of heaven" (Matt. xviii. 1-3). So He allayed the animosity of His ten apostles over the ambitious desire of the sons of Zebedee, James and John, by the touching rule: " Ye know that the princes of the Gentiles exercise dominion over them, and they that are great exercise authority upon them; but it shall not be so among you; but whosoever will be great among you, let him be your minister, and whosoever will be chief among you, let him be your servant; even as the Son of Man came not to be ministered unto, but to minister, and to give His life a ransom for many" (Matt. xx. 25-28). Now, the connection of the Church with the State tends decidedly to foster the propensities which these commandments condemn. It invests one Church with ascendency over the others. It attaches the seal of State-authority to the doctrine, the form of worship, the organization of one Church, with the necessary consequence of setting the other churches in the condition of being suffered to exist, but not approved. It concentrates the sunshine of the State's favour on one Church, and consequently puts the other churches in the shade. It gives to the State-Church the influence and the social prestige of standing in a special connection with the Crown, of having an exalted representation in the House of Lords, of being all through the land the especial representative and maintainer of State-law and State-government, and brings thereby upon the millions of British subjects, who do not belong to the State-Church, but are as loyal to the Crown, and as law-abiding as the members of the State-Church, the undeserved imputation of less attachment to the law and the great disadvantage of social inferiority. The whole tendency, therefore, of the connection of the Church with the State is to promote the feeling of worldly ascendency in the Church, and to gratify the worldly passion for influence and dominion. This danger is especially great in England because the Norman Conquest has introduced in English society the relation between the different classes of conquerors with their rights of dominion and superiority, and of conquered with their duties of submission—a relation which, however modified in the course of centuries by the interests of the conquerors and the energy of the conquered, by the intermingling of the two classes, by the course of political events, and the spirit of the age; however disguised under the modern names of aristocracy and democracy, of ruling classes and of ruled, of upper ten thousand and common millions, because the former relation is felt to be out of date, and to have lost its right of existence, is still in many respects sufficiently influential to make itself felt in the tone and manners of English social life. Now, no relation can be found more alien to the Spirit and the Word of Christ, and therefore more opposite to the character and duty of Christ's Church than this, and still there exists in England in the present day no institution which tends so much to keep this relation alive and working than the connection of the Episcopal Church with the State, by providing in the State-Church an organization for the social ascendency of its members, that, bound up with the powerful agencies of religion, made itself felt throughout the whole land.

The connection of the Church with the State, while exalting the worldly position of the Church, hinders her from arriving at the full consciousness of the dignity to which Christ has called the ministers and members of His Church. The ministers of His Church He has charged to be His ambassadors (2 Cor. v. 20), receiving their commission and their authority from Him; to be guided exclusively by His Word and His Spirit; to set forth not only His gospel, but His life in the world, depending as Christ Himself did when on earth, for blessing and success upon their work, not on the influences of earthly greatness, but on the power of the truth and the blessing of God. Now, without intending in the least to disparage the character of the present occupant of the See of Canterbury, who has shown in the creation of the Bishop of London's Fund to know how to work in the spirit of the head of a free Episcopal Church, the position of the Archbishop of Canterbury is less fit to realize this vocation of Christ's ministers, than the position of the most obscure minister of the poorest Methodist connection in the remotest corner of the land. The position of the Archbishop of Canterbury is exceedingly fit to attract men not at all distinguished by divine vocation, while the position of the obscure Methodist minister has nothing to attract save those who feel themselves divinely called to preach the gospel. The Archbishop of Canterbury is nominated by instrumentalities not at all possessing the guarantees that they will be led in their choice only by the influences of Christ's Spirit, while the Methodist minister is chosen under the invocation of the guidance from on high, by Church-influences most likely to choose the man of Christ's intention. The Archbishop of Canterbury has to occupy a social position, which makes it exceedingly difficult, if not impossible, to be nothing else in his work and in his life, but a representative of the crucified Nazarene, acting in His spirit, reflecting His image, using His means, walking in His ways, while no such impediments exist for the obscure Methodist minister. The Archbishop of Canterbury has, in the exercise of his work, to consider besides God's Word and the guidance of God's Spirit, so many statutes and judgments of lawyers and customs and demands of those in high places and social influences and State- or Court-intrigues, that it becomes well-nigh impossible, as the servant of Christ, to mind nothing but the will of His Master, and that will in its full extent; while the Methodist minister finds in his position very little to hinder and very much to compel him to be guided by Christ's Spirit, and to make it his watchword: " Nothing but the Bible, the Bible alone, the Bible entirely !" While, therefore, the social position of the Primate is incomparably more exalted, the position of the most obscure Dissenting minister is really more honourable for the minister of Christ's Church, being more in harmony with the character of his work and with the Spirit of Christ.

The same is true with regard to the Church-members. Christ's disciples are made by Christ kings and priests unto God His Father (Apoc. i. 6; v. 10; 1 Peter ii. 9), in all things concerning the salvation of their souls and the kingdom of heaven, called to be free from all creature-authority, only to be subject willingly and unreservedly to Christ, with free access (unrestrained by any law-precepts with regard to the forms) to the most intimate fellowship with their Father in heaven, through the only mediation of Christ by the Spirit (Eph. ii. 18;

1 Tim. ii. 1–6; Heb. iv. 14–16; vii. 25; x. 19–22), and as they live in the Spirit, so to walk in the Spirit. Now, while believers within the Free Churches have nothing in their Church-organization to impede the full realization of the measure of glory to which they, through the unspeakable richness of their Saviour's grace, are called, and may glory in the liberty wherewith Christ has made them free, find believers within the State-Church, in the connection with the State, which distinguishes their Church in an earthly sense, a serious impediment to living in the full exercise of the privileges of Christ's disciples. They have to look not only to the good pleasure of their heavenly King, but also to the dictates of the State and its laws, with respect to the interests of their Church-life, and to submit the moving of God's Spirit in their hearts to the control of agencies, not led only, if at all, by the influence of Christ. They allow themselves to be subject, with regard to their spiritual interest and their Church, to the powers of this world, and forfeit thereby the enjoyment of the royal privilege which their Saviour bought for them at the cost of His blood, and mar the influence of the Holy Ghost dwelling in them, who is jealous of His right upon undivided allegiance and upon being acknowledged as the Spirit of a royal priesthood, through Him partaking of the honours of their heavenly Head, Christ.

Moreover, the repugnance of the sinful human heart against submission to the authority of God brought home to the heart in the influences of His Spirit, and its blindness to the things of the Spirit, make it prone to follow in religion the dictates of some spurious authority, that of necessity must confound it in the hour of need. Therefore the fundamental command of the Good Shepherd to all who are to be His true sheep is: "Follow Me; My sheep hear My voice, and I know them, and they follow Me" (John x. 27); "If any man will come after Me, let him deny himself, and take up his cross and follow Me" (Matt. xvi. 24), and as a decisive characteristic of God's children is named by the Apostle Paul (Rom. viii. 14): "As many as are led by the Spirit of God, they are the sons of God;" and their vocation traced out in the words (Gal. v. 25): "If we live in the Spirit, let us also walk in the Spirit." But the State-connections, encompassing the State-Church with the halo of State-authority, which is more akin to the disposition of the sinful human heart than the authority of God's Spirit, tends to strengthen the carnal tendencies of the heart, to estrange it more from the influence of the Spirit; to make it content to be led by State-authority instead of by the Spirit of God; to entice it to rest in the acceptance of what is good in what is imposed by State-authority, not on the authority of God, but on the authority of men, hindering thereby the vital truth from exerting its influence on the heart and life; leading to the acceptance of error as well as truth, bad as well as good, while covered by the authority of the incompetent State, and by accustoming the mind to lean on men's authority in the vital interests of their souls, to prepare the way to the acceptance of the authority of the pretendedly infallible Roman Pope. Not to the voice of Jesus, nor to the dictates of the Spirit, but to the enactments of State-laws, made without decisive influence of the Word of God, is the heart directed in the vital questions of salvation, these being unable to supply what it wants, to satisfy its needs in life and death, and before the judgment-seat of God, and creating thereby the awful danger of the most terrible disappointment in the highest interests of the human soul.

Another dangerous tendency is to still the cravings after religion, with which it has pleased God to distinguish human nature, with the stolid rest under some imposed religious organizations and the heartless performance of some prepared form of religious worship while sin remains unchecked in the heart. The whole tendency, on the contrary, of Christ's Word and influence is to oppose the pharisaical attachment to imposed religious forms, and to make religion a soul-stirring, heart-renewing and life-hallowing power, which can be only true when affecting and shaping man's deepest individual experience and life. Jesus' word to Nicodemus: "Verily, verily, I say unto thee, Except a man be born of water and of the Spirit, he cannot enter into the kingdom of God" (John iii. 5); to the Samaritan woman: "The hour cometh, and now is, when the true worshippers shall worship the Father in spirit and in truth: for the Father seeketh such to worship Him" (John iv. 23) and the parables of the pearl of great price and of the treasure hidden in the field (Matt. xiii. 44, 45), are sufficient to establish the truth of what is to be found on every page of the New Testament. Now in all religious organizations there is a danger of religion being an outwardly imposed form, rather than an inward living power; but while Free Churches, organized on the principle of personal faith in Christ and voluntary dedication to His cause, have, in the principle of their organization, the proper antidote against that danger, the connection of the State with the Church has the tendency to strengthen that danger by imposing the State-Church organizations, worship, and doctrine, with the outward authority of the State-law, and thereby promoting the fatal error of the worldly heart, that religion belongs to the domain fit to be regulated by State-laws, that is, of earthly interests and outward forms.

Another tendency of the sinful nature of man is to mingle different forms of worldliness with the worship of God; to let earthly distinctions exercise their influence within the House of God; to apply an earthly standard of man's worth within the sphere of the Church and to aim at earthly advantages in his service of God. The dictates of God's Word are: "No man can serve two masters: for either he will hate the one, and love the other; or else he will hold to

AN APPEAL TO THE CONSCIENCE. 69

the one, and despise the other. Ye cannot serve God and mammon" (Matt. vi. 24); "Know ye not that the friendship of the world is enmity with God? Whosoever therefore will be a friend of the world is the enemy of God" (James iv. 4); "Love not the world, neither the things that are in the world. If any man love the world, the love of the Father is not in him. For all that is in the world, the lust of the flesh and the lust of the eyes and the pride of life, is not of the Father, but is of the world. And the world passeth away and the lust thereof: but he that doeth the will of God abideth for ever (1 John ii. 15-17); "God is no respecter of persons; but in every nation he that feareth Him, and worketh righteousness is accepted with Him (Acts x. 34, 35); "My brethren, have not the faith of our Lord Jesus Christ, the Lord of glory, with respect of persons. For if there come unto your assembly a man with a gold ring, in goodly apparel, and there come in also a poor man in vile raiment; and ye have respect to him that weareth the gay clothing, and say unto him: Sit thou here in a good place; and say to the poor: Stand thou there, or sit here under my footstool: are ye not then partial in yourselves, and are become judges of evil thoughts? Hearken, my beloved brethren, Hath not God chosen the poor of this world rich in faith, and heirs of the kingdom which He hath promised to them that love Him" (James ii. 1-5, 9)? "From such as suppose that gain is godliness withdraw thyself; but godliness with contentment is great gain. For we brought nothing into this world, and it is certain we can carry nothing out. And having food and raiment let us be therewith content. But they that will be rich fall into temptation and a snare, and into many foolish and hurtful lusts, which drown men in destruction and perdition" (1 Tim. vi. 5–9). Now the connection with the State, in direct opposition to these commandments, introduces all kind of worldly considerations in the Church's life. Attaching State-honours to Church-officers, State-authority and State-influences to Church-organization, it promotes the principle of worldly distinctions in the Church's estimation of men. It necessitates that a man's place in the Church is not regulated by the depth of his piety, the strength of his faith, the power of his love, the holiness and energy of his influence, but by his earthly connections, his social influence, and the amount of Governmental favour he possesses. Attributing legal, judicial, and administrative power over the Church's affairs to the State-authorities, it leads in the promotion of the Church's interests not in the first place to look to the will of Christ, nor to the dictates of His Spirit, but to the disposition of the Government of the day and the number of Parliamentary votes over which it can dispose; and, consequently, instead of using the only proper spiritual means, to stoop to the intricacies of political intrigue. Preferring the advantage of social prestige and State-favour to Church-fellowship, it feeds rather than extinguishes the love of the world, that so easily spoils and paralyzes all true religious life.

The sinful human heart is deceitful above all things, consequently no injunction is more frequently made in the Word of God than to love the truth in the different spheres of life. Now, the connection with the State places the Church in a false position, leaving her, as we have shown, the name of Church, but destroying her true Church-organization, and setting in the place under the Church-name a State-institution for worship and for the promotion of religious interests among the people, that includes the most heterogeneous elements, and finds its bond of unity rather in State-laws, form of worship and of government, than in the indwelling of the Holy Ghost. The consequence is, that while the wish to retain the connection with the State at all costs is very strongly and very generally fostered, all kind of theories about the character and the duties of the Church are tried in order to find a plausible defence for the union of Church and State. The entering on an earnest inquiry into the true nature of the Church and her connection with the State is instinctively avoided, and a set purpose manifested to maintain it against the clearest arguments. The judgment is warped by prejudice, and where no escape remains by argument from acknowledging the impropriety of the union, the contest often terminates with a haughty or angry appeal to the authority of the law, whose right of existence is exactly the point in question.

For all these reasons, there can be no reasonable doubt that the connection of the Church with the State tends to counteract the influence of God's Spirit in the hearts of believing Church people, and that it is consequently the will of Christ, that this evil shall not be allowed to continue.

III.

The connection of the Church with the State is also an impediment against the coming of God's kingdom in the world.

The whole argument hitherto exposed, that that connection is against the fundamental principles of the kingdom of heaven and counteracts the influence of God's Spirit upon the hearts of believers, is one continual proof of what we have here to establish; but we wish here, in two additional particulars, to show how it hinders the spread of Christianity in our time.

Nothing is more characteristic of our time in the sphere of religion, than that materialistic tendencies, more or less consequently developed, estrange the hearts of many—chiefly among well-educated men—from Christianity. They do not believe in the reality and power of God and the spiritual agencies of His kingdom. Not a few deny them openly and boldly, and try to form a rule of life in accordance with their infidelity. But a great many more, though theoretically still holding a superficial belief of the truth of God's existence and of Christianity, are practically atheists—God and Christ have no real place in their lives. The resources of human power and wisdom, the results of natural science, the achievements of industry, the products of literature and art fill their thoughts, attract their desires, shape their life, form the basis of their calculations and the sphere of their pleasures. They have lost their earnest belief in the reality of the supernatural and its dominion over the natural. Nothing tends more to strengthen them in their unbelief than the inconsistency of those who profess to believe in Christ, manifested in living not by faith but upon the principles of a materialistic creed; while, on the other hand, no argument makes so much impression upon them as a life of which simple earnest faith in God is the principle. But in the State-Church they witness an institution which professes in its confession and worship to believe in God, in salvation through Christ, and in the power of His Spirit; that in many of its agencies works to bring others to the same belief, but submit and cleave in its connections with the State to a power belonging to the same outward, earthly sphere in which the roots of materialistic life are laid; guided by the same considerations and motives, trusting on the same kind of resources and influences, courting the same kind of advantages which shape and fill the materialistic life; and the effect which this inconsistency produces is to lead them to the conviction that the Church is not in earnest in her profession of belief in God and His kingdom, but continues in it because it suits her to adhere to old superstitions. The inconsistency of the Church, manifested in her cleaving to her connection with the State, counteracts, therefore, the converting influences which in other respects she seeks to bring to bear against the infidel, and erects a new impediment against his acceptance of Christ.

One of the most dangerous parasites of religious life is the tendency to partake from worldly motives in religious performances. It is worldliness in its worst form, destroying all reverence for God and His service, made secure by the hypocritical appearance of performing the highest duty. Now this wretched iniquity is systematically promoted by the connection of the Church with the State. The worldly advantages, the social influence and prestige emanating from it, are the most powerful inducements for the worldly heart to join the State-Church and its services. Greedy love of money finds, in the relation with the State-Church, a successful recommendation to the commercial favours of the rich; or at least a means for satisfying the claims of their conscience for some religion without much cost. Snobbish cravings for social contact with, and gracious acknowledgment by, the upper-classes of society, see in marked zeal for the State-connection and the worship of the State-Church, a welcome bridge to what they seek. Lofty ambition finds in the steady and close adherence to the religious agencies of the State-Church, most suitable steps to the favours of powerful patronage and to attractive advancement. The most earnest and faithful pastoral and church-labours of the State-Church-clergy, aiming at the promotion of truly spiritual piety among the people, without any intention of using influences emanating from the State-connection of their Church, have, by the fact of their belonging to the State-Church, thrown round their labours an atmosphere of wordly advantages through their connection with the State, which seriously endangers in all cases, and in not a few really destroys the intended fruit of their labours, by inducing people to comply with their demands of Church-going, Bible-reading, partaking of Sacraments, etc., for the sake of the worldly advantages, resulting from the connection of the Church with the State.

But there is one of the strongest arguments generally advanced for the continuance of the existing connection of the Church with the State, which has respect to this part of the subject, namely, that through it Church-agencies are in many places sustained where, but for it, they would not exist. The State-connection, it is contended, by dividing out the kingdom into parishes, gives every individual a right to the offices of the parish-clergyman which but for State-endowment could in many places not be found. But this argument rests on an asserted superiority of the power of official compulsion above the influence of voluntary love, which can neither stand the test of present experience, nor of history, nor of the Bible. Recent statistics, officially or privately gathered, set it beyond all doubt that in the last quarter of a century the religious agencies of Free Churches have been multiplied throughout the land on a much larger scale than those of the State-Church; and experience proves that the ministers of the Free Churches, though not bound by State-law, are never found wanting, when a person solicits their aid; while from the nature of the case, the service given from voluntary motives is much more valuable than that administered simply from a sense of official responsibility. Among the efforts for the unprovided part of the population, made during the last few years within the State-Church, those of the Bishop of London's Fund are devised and executed, not on the principle of State-endowments, but of free-will contributions. The history of the Free Church of Scotland is in itself sufficient to prove the entire groundlessness of the proffered argument. Entirely from free-will offerings it has covered Scotland, even in its remotest corners, with a large number of churches, manses, and fairly well-sustained ministers and religious agencies, providing, besides, respectable funds for different church and home and foreign missionary objects, and has thereby, during an existence of over thirty years, furnished a noble living proof of what the history of the other Free Churches in England, Scotland, the United States and elsewhere testifies, that the simple voluntary principle has sufficient vitality to provide for the religious wants of the world.

If ever the voluntary principle had to encounter stupendous difficulties, it was certainly in the first three centuries of the Christian Church; and, as has been already shown, the kingdom of Christ was established in the world, in spite of the most powerful State-opposition, entirely on the voluntary principle, deriving from the exercise of it additional freshness, strength, and zeal of love, that could not be quenched in the fire of pagan and Romish persecution. Moreover, the argument is nothing but a disguised indictment of the principles of Christ Himself, as revealed in the Gospel. When commissioning His apostles for their first mission, He instructs them to rely only on the voluntary principle, that is, in other words, on Him who sends them, for the provision of their wants, in saying— "Provide neither gold nor silver nor brass in your purses, nor scrip for your journey, neither two coats, neither shoes, nor yet staves: for the workman is worthy of his meat" (Matt. x. 9, 10). While the whole of the New Testament is one great testimony to the truth that the power which is only able to conquer the world is simple, living faith, that by bringing the heart under the power of the love of God in Christ, engenders and sustains that voluntary obedience to God and His will, which is far more powerful and rich in resources than the mightiest State-influence.

What the argument proves, is not that the connection of the Church with the State is beneficial for the promotion of the coming of God's kingdom, but that it has the effect of so far stifling the noble impulses of Christianity, that Church-members dare pretend that the power of State-help is mightier than the power of Christ's influence, unconscious that in so doing they deny the vital principles of Christianity.

And now having proved that the connection of the Church with the State is against the fundamental principles of the kingdom of heaven, counteracts the working of God's Spirit in the hearts of believers, and is an impediment to the coming of God's kingdom in the world, and therefore against the will of Christ, I wish in conclusion to direct an earnest appeal to the consciences of all who in the State-Church care for the will of their Saviour, to ponder in their closets before the eyes of their Lord and Saviour what is brought under their notice in this tract, with all the earnestness that the nature of the case demands, following the noble example of those of Berea, " searching the Scriptures, whether these things are true" (Acts xvii. 11); and if, as I think will be the case, they find them true in the main, not to allow the power of prejudice, nor the spell of long-venerated traditions, nor the attraction of highly cherished associations, nor the deceitfulness of worldly advantages to beguile them from the plain path of duty, but to resolve, with the help of Christ, from henceforth to do what they can, by their prayers and their active efforts, to remove what is a snare for their own souls, which mars the life and the usefulness of their Church, which is a rankling sore in England's social life, and which dishonours the Lord Jesus, and to set the Episcopal Church in England free from her improper connection with the State.

And my Nonconformist brethren I wish earnestly to beseech, under full appreciation of what they have already done and are doing for the promotion of the disestablishment of the State-Church, to elevate and to keep the disestablishment-movement mainly above all considerations of expediency and convenience to the domain of the conscience, that finds in the establishment of the State-Church the vital principles of God's truth, the deepest interests of the State-Church herself and of God's kingdom, the honour of Christ at stake, in order to make the promotion of the disestablishment of the State-Church what it ought to be, the work of the noblest impulses of their Christian hearts, chiefly of that Christ-like, soul-expanding love that seeketh not her own, and thereby the cause of God, that they may be able with regard to it in simple, but energetic faith, to lay hold on the almighty influence of God's arm and Spirit, and in His power to remove this mountain from the path of England's Christianity, and thus be the means, without opening perpetual sores in Christian hearts, of clearing the English social atmosphere of an element most detrimental to Christian fellowship; to promote personal piety among Churchmen and Dissenters, and the triumph of true spiritual religion over worldliness, superstition, imperiousness, egoism and unbelief, to the joy of Christ and to the honour of God.

www.ingramcontent.com/pod-product-compliance
Lightning Source LLC
Chambersburg PA
CBHW020324090426
42735CB00009B/1389